# Rain

Andres Llamas Ruiz

*Illustrations by Luis Rizo*

**Sterling Publishing Co., Inc.**
New York

Illustrations by Luis Rizo
Text by Andres Llamas Ruiz
Translated by Natalia Tizón

**Library of Congress Cataloging-in-Publication Data**

Llamas Ruiz, Andrés.
  [Lluvia. English]
  Rain / Andres Llamas Ruiz.
      p.      cm. — (Sequences of earth & space)
  Includes index.
  Summary: Provides an introduction to weather phenomena
associated with rain, including clouds, fronts, atmospheric pres-
sure, thunder and lightning, and more.
  ISBN 0-8069-9333-2
  1. Rain and rainfall—Juvenile literature.   [1.  Rain and rainfall.
2. Weather.]   I. Title.   II. Series: Llamas Ruiz, Andrés.
Secuencias de la tierra y el espacio.   English.
QC924.7.L5713   1996
551.55—dc20                                        96–25866
                                                      CIP
                                                       AC


1   3   5   7   9   10   8   6   4   2

Published by Sterling Publishing Company, Inc.
387 Park Avenue South, New York, N.Y. 10016
Originally published in Spain by Ediciones Estes
©1995 by Ediciones Estes, S.A.
English version and translation © 1996 by Sterling Publishing Company, Inc.
Distributed in Canada by Sterling Publishing
℅ Canadian Manda Group, One Atlantic Avenue, Suite 105
Toronto, Ontario, Canada M6K 3E7
Distributed in Great Britain and Europe by Cassell PLC
Wellington House, 125 Strand, London WC2R 0BB, England
Distributed in Australia by Capricorn Link (Australia) Pty Ltd.
P.O. Box 6651, Baulkham Hills, Business Centre, NSW 2153, Australia
*Printed and Bound in Spain*
*All rights reserved*

Sterling  ISBN 0-8069-9333-2

# Table of Contents

# Water Evaporation

Where does rainwater come from?

Roughly 457,450 million cubic yards (350,000 million cubic meters) of water evaporate from the earth each year. Approximately the same amount then falls back down to earth as rain and snow.

Everything begins with the sun. The energy in the sun's rays heats the water, melting snow and ice, and transforms it into tiny molecules of a gas called water vapor. The vapor then rises up into the atmosphere.

While you cannot actually see evaporation, the process does produce some outward signs. For example, when water vapor is present in the atmosphere, it produces a haze, or fog.

*Plants lose water through transpiration (vapors passing through pores). The more plant life there is in an area, the more water vapor forms.*

Here, you can see how evaporation takes place from different points of the earth's surface. Most of the total atmospheric humidity (85% of it) originates from evaporation of seawater; the rest is the result of plant transpiration and evaporation of water from rivers, lakes, and land.

The atmosphere retains part of the heat reflected from the earth's surface. This is called the "greenhouse effect," and it ensures that the earth does not cool down too much when it is not receiving the sun's rays, such as at night.

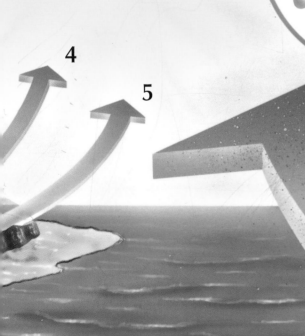

6

4

5

1. Evaporation from snow and ice.

2. Evaporation from plants.

3. Evaporation from pools and lakes.

4. Evaporation from rivers and streams.

5. Evaporation of water from the earth's surface.

6. Detail of water vapor molecules.

# Atmospheric Pressure

What happens to water vapor that reaches the atmosphere?

When it reaches the atmosphere, water vapor encounters a very complex system of large, independent air masses that cover thousands of square miles and reach far into the sky.

The phrase "atmospheric pressure" refers to the mass of air in the atmosphere that is weighing down on the earth. The pressure on the earth's surface is normally 1.033 kg/cm² (=760 millimeters, or 29.64 inches of mercury, or 1013 millibars), which means that everybody on earth is bearing a weight of 2,000 pounds (900 kilos)! We don't notice the weight of the air because it exerts pressure on us from all sides at once.

Nevertheless, pressure varies because it depends on the characteristics of the mass of air above. In some areas, pressure exceeds 29.64 inches (1013 mb): these are high-pressure zones or "anticyclones," where it is usually good weather. Other areas have lower pressure: these are the low-pressure zones or depressions (storms) and they cause bad weather.

1

On a sunny summer's day when there are few clouds in the sky, the sun's rays meet no obstacles and reach the earth's surface with all their energy intact. On an overcast day, the clouds filter out over 80% of the sun's heat.

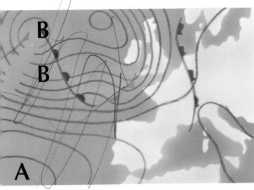

A

Isobars are lines that connect areas of equal pressure on a map. To make a weather forecast, it is necessary to observe the high-pressure areas (A: anticyclone) and the low-pressure areas (B: storm).

At the right, you can see how in each hemisphere of the planet three large air masses form: the Arctic, polar, and tropical air masses.

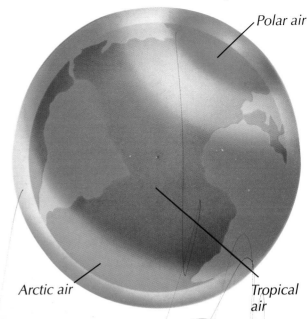

Polar air

Arctic air

Tropical air

A

B

Barometers are used to measure atmospheric pressure. **A.** If the weather is good and the barometer's needle quickly drops, it means that it will rain. **B.** If the weather is good and the needle drops slowly but steadily, good weather will continue.

2

A sunny day (1) is very stable; the dawn is clear and it normally remains sunny. Clouds only build up when there is sufficient humidity in the air and enough movement in the layers of air to enable the humidity to ascend into the atmosphere (2).

# The Wind Gets Up

After water vapor has ascended into the atmosphere, where does it go?

That depends on the winds. Once they have built up, air masses do not remain motionless. Instead they travel, changing their characteristics as they go. For example, if a mass of dry air moves over the sea, it will pick up a lot of humidity. If the wind tousles your hair, you are, in fact, in the way of a traveling air mass!

Winds are caused by differences in air pressure. Air masses move from areas of high pressure (anticyclones) toward areas of low pressure (depressions).

The hot air near the equator tends to rise because it is light and warm. On the other hand, near the poles, cold and dense air masses form. These tend to descend and move away from the poles toward zones at the equator. Since cold air is heavier than warm air, descending cold air causes high pressure, while ascending warm air causes low pressure.

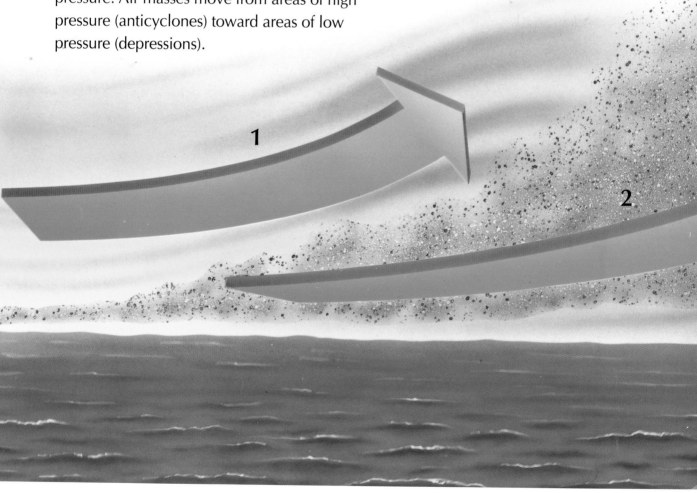

When the wind begins to blow, air masses begin journeys that can cover hundreds of miles. The weather in any particular area depends on the nature of the air mass in the atmosphere above. The direction of the wind and

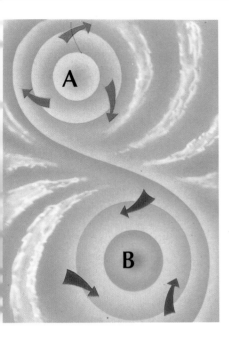

A

B

*Air always moves from anticyclone (A) to storm (B).*

*At the right, you can see how the cold air at the poles travels toward the equator and vice-versa. Nevertheless, the rotation of the earth influences and complicates the picture and creates three different convection cells in each hemisphere.*

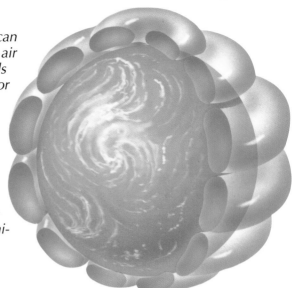

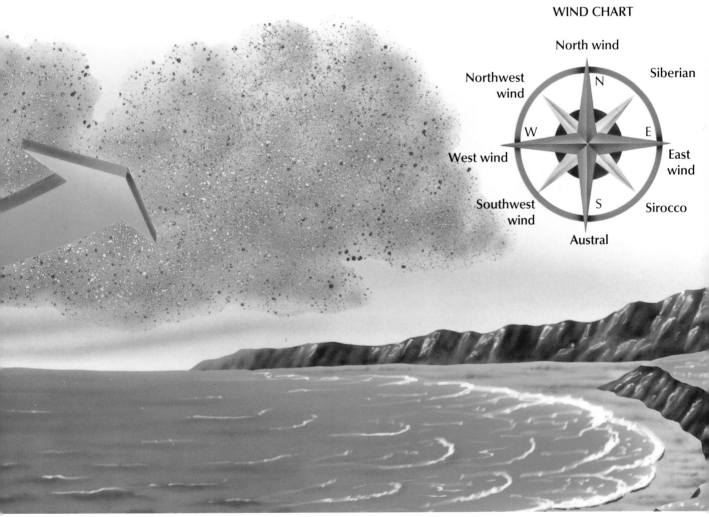

**WIND CHART**

North wind

Northwest wind

Siberian

West wind

East wind

Southwest wind

Sirocco

Austral

the weather are closely related. For example, in mid-latitudes, westerly winds normally bring rain and storms because the wind blows west to east.

**1.** Wind blows from high-pressure areas to low-pressure areas.

**2.** Water vapor.

# A Front Forms

Where does bad weather come from?

Normally, it is caused by depressions, above all in the winter. We have already seen that air masses are moved around by winds and that two different air masses may bump into each other. When masses of warm and cold air meet, the line of contact is called a front. The actual line is not vertical because cold air weighs more and tends to slide in under the warm air. There are two main types of front: the cold front and the warm front.

Many depressions originate over the oceans: Masses of cold, dry polar air meet masses of warm, humid tropical air. A depression forms as warm tropical air rises over cold polar air, creating an area of low pressure. As a result, winds begin to revolve around the center of the low-pressure area, forming a warm front and a cold front.

Here you see how a depression forms: **1.** A polar front forms when warm tropical air hits cold polar air.

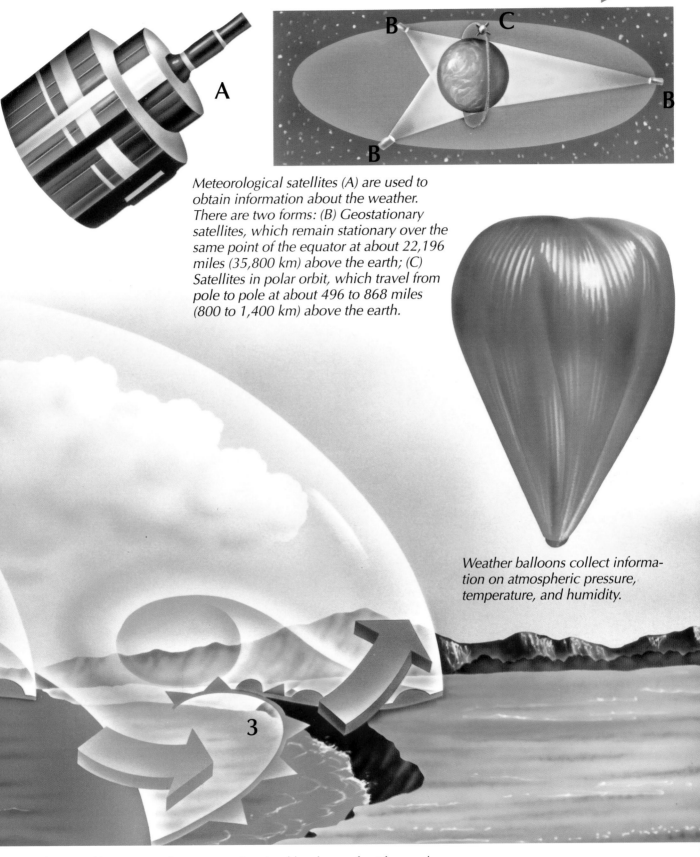

Meteorological satellites (A) are used to obtain information about the weather. There are two forms: (B) Geostationary satellites, which remain stationary over the same point of the equator at about 22,196 miles (35,800 km) above the earth; (C) Satellites in polar orbit, which travel from pole to pole at about 496 to 868 miles (800 to 1,400 km) above the earth.

Weather balloons collect information on atmospheric pressure, temperature, and humidity.

**2.** An area of low pressure forms, around which the two air masses, pushed by the Coriolis force, begin to spin.

**3.** A cold and warm front form and they begin to move eastward.

# The Buildup of Clouds

How does water vapor form clouds?

Usually, the air is full of water in the form of water vapor. When it cools sufficient-`ly, it condenses into small droplets to form clouds, mists, or hazes. Air cools most frequently when it rises and expands.

As the air cools, the humidity within condenses because the cooler the air is, the less water vapor it can hold. Eventually, the air cools down to the "dew point," beyond which it cannot hold any more water vapor.

Then, the vapor condenses into tiny water droplets. Now you can see the cloud! However, water vapor only forms droplets if it can find sufficient solid particles to condense around. These particles may be made of dust, smoke, pollen, sea salt, etc. They are known as "condensation nuclei."

*On the right, the condensation of water vapor around a particle of dust, pollen, or sea salt.*

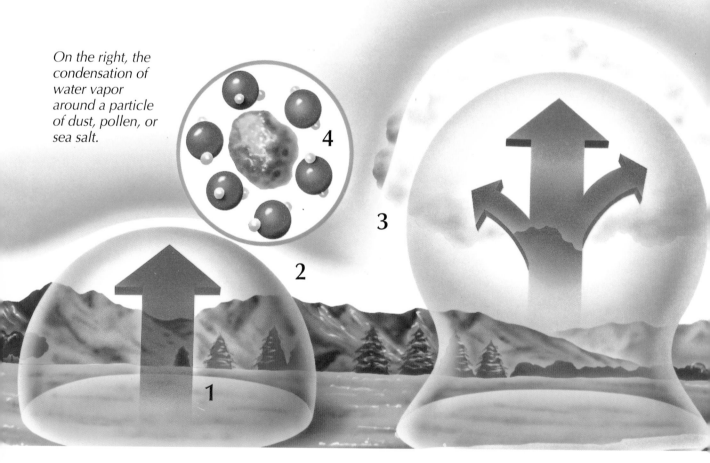

Clouds appear when air cools to below the dew point and water vapor condenses into small droplets.

**1.** A warm area of the earth's surface heats the air above it.

**2.** A bubble of warm air forms and slowly rises.

**A**
**B**
**C**

*Cumulus clouds form when the sun's rays heat the earth, causing the air above to heat up and rise. This humid air rises into an area of cooler air and the water vapor condenses and forms a cloud.*

**A. Cirrus:** *Small, high, long, and thin clouds made up of minute ice crystals.*
**B . Cirrostratus:** *Very fine layers of ice crystals.*
**C. Cirrocumulus:** *Raindrops become ice crystals when they reach a certain height.*

5

**3.** As it rises, the air expands and cools.

**4.** When the air bubble has cooled, water vapor forms droplets of water around the condensation nuclei.

**5.** A cloud forms.

# A Front Approaches

As a depression approaches, a warm front—loaded with warm, moist tropical air—is usually the first front to appear. This air condenses and forms clouds as it rises above a wedge of cold polar air. As the warm front approaches, atmospheric pressure falls quickly and constantly; the temperature and humidity rise; visibility diminishes; and the wind freshens, swinging from south to southwest. (In the southern hemisphere, wind changes occur the other way around.)

If you keep your eye on the sky, you will see long streaks of cirrus clouds forming. These clouds warn us that the depression is about to arrive. Then, as the warm front moves over, the streaks of cirrus are replaced by a milky veil of cirrostratus—a sure sign that rain is on its way.

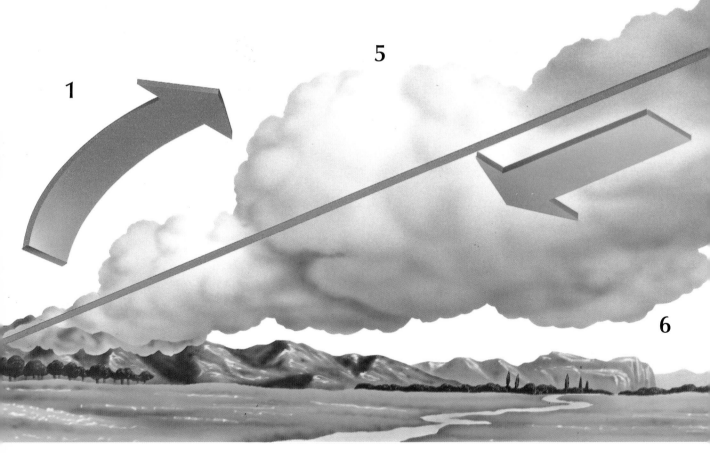

Here, you can see the sequence of events that occur as the warm front of a depression passes over.

1. The warm air rises over the cold air.
2. Long, thread-like cirrus clouds form.

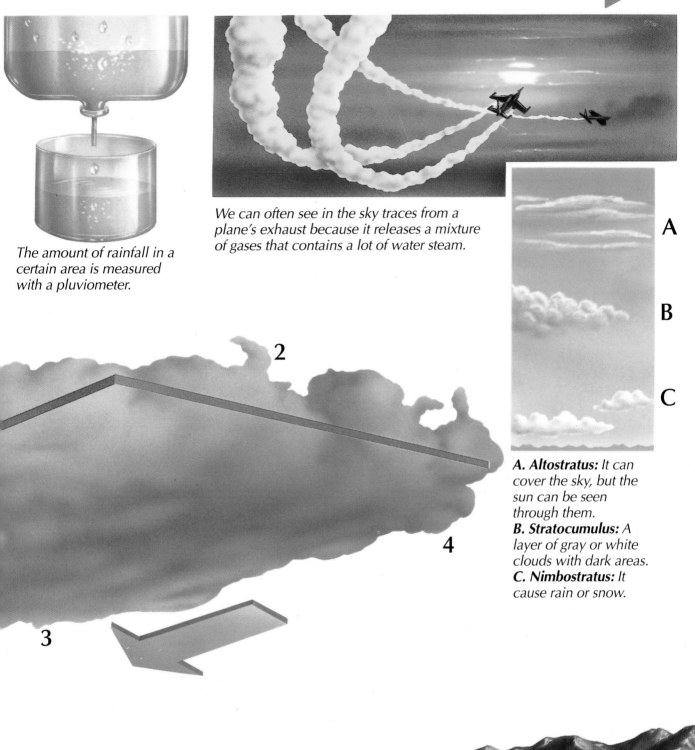

The amount of rainfall in a certain area is measured with a pluviometer.

We can often see in the sky traces from a plane's exhaust because it releases a mixture of gases that contains a lot of water steam.

2

3

4

A

B

C

**A. Altostratus:** It can cover the sky, but the sun can be seen through them.
**B. Stratocumulus:** A layer of gray or white clouds with dark areas.
**C. Nimbostratus:** It cause rain or snow.

**3.** The cirrostratus signal that it is going to rain.

**4.** It normally rains first in this area.
**5.** The altostratus clouds usually bring the first rain.

**6.** The cold air passes under the warm air.

# The Rain Begins to Fall

What exactly happens inside a cloud when it begins to rain?

The millions and millions of water droplets and ice particles or crystals that form a cloud are so small that they have to grow to be able to fall as rain. This can occur by condensation or by coalescence. Condensation normally occurs inside clouds containing water and ice particles. If the cloud rises so high that the temperature drops below freezing, many water droplets freeze and ice crystals form. These crystals gradually increase in size and, within a few minutes, turn into snowflakes that begin to fall through the cloud.

As the snowflakes pass through warmer layers of air, they melt and form warmer drops, which fall as rain.

When water droplets in clouds grow to 0.004 of an inch (.1 mm ) in diameter, they begin to fall as rain because rising air currents can no longer keep them in suspension. Raindrops often grow to have diameters of between 0.04 and 0.2 of an inch (1 and 5 mm). The heaviest rains are caused by the tallest and

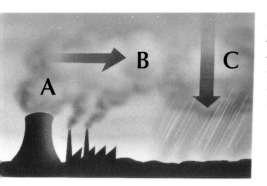

*Particles of pollution are released into the atmosphere (A). They can be transported by the wind (B), or fall as acid rain (C).*

*Where water is scarce, rain can be artificially provoked by "seeding" clouds with chemicals from planes and rockets. This method only works when there is a lot of water vapor present in the clouds.*

*The water droplets are pushed upward by air currents and bump into one another. Big particles absorb the smaller, and when they grow large enough, they fall as rain (as shown on the left).*

darkest clouds, which have sufficient height for large numbers of big water droplets to form.

**1.** Formation of raindrops: a) Coalescence—due to the collision of little raindrops. b) Ice crystals melt as they warm up.

# The Warm Front Passes Over

When a warm front passes overhead, rain may last for several hours. Drizzle and showers fall continually and visibility is very bad.

As the front passes, atmospheric pressure stops falling, the temperature rises a little, and the humidity increases quite sharply. The wind may pick up a little and the sky is covered by a nimbostratus.

At this point, there is a short interval before the cold front arrives. It is as if the bad weather wants to have a break; the weather improves as atmospheric pressure drops—more slowly than before—and the wind loses force. The steady rain turns to drizzle and the nimbostratus is replaced by a stratocumulus and stratus. Clouds begin to disperse and eventually disappear altogether! However, appearances can be deceiving...

The weather improves after the warm front has passed. Nevertheless, it's time to seek shelter because the arrival of the cold front is imminent.

1. The nimbostratus disappears and is replaced by the stratus and stratocumulus.

*A tornado is a "funnel" up to 660 feet (200 meters) high. In the center, there is a powerful updraft, and on the outside there is a current of ascending air that sucks in and destroys everything in its path.*

**2.** Clear patches begin to appear in the sky.

**3.** The rain stops briefly.

**4.** Poor visibility continues.

**5.** Relative humidity rises quickly.

# The Cold Front Arrives

The calm that follows a warm front is suddenly interrupted by the arrival of thick, threatening cumulonimbus clouds, which tell us that the cold front has arrived.

The temperature has fallen rapidly and it is now much colder. You'll also notice that the wind has changed direction and is now coming from the west or northwest, instead of from the southeast. If you look at the barometer, you'll see that the atmospheric pressure is rising rapidly.

However, the most characteristic feature of the cold front is heavy rain—storms that build up when cold air forces warm air to rise quickly. These storms unleash large quantities of water and hail, although they do not usually last for more than an hour. You'll notice that during this period visibility improves a lot.

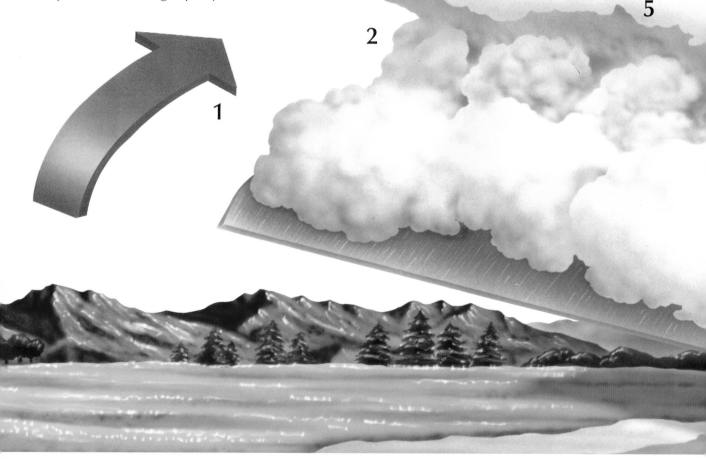

The cold front brings with it strong winds, large dark clouds, and heavy rain.

1. Strong, gusty winds blow toward the front.
2. Warm air rises quickly.

Hail forms inside cumulonimbus clouds. Strong air currents force water droplets to ascend to the higher layers of the cloud. There, they freeze and descend until they are forced up again by the air currents and the process is repeated over and over again.

A

B

C

1. **Altocumulus:** *Cotton-wool clouds that announce bad weather.*
2. **Cumulus:** *Round, white clouds that indicate good weather.*
3. **Cumulonimbus:** *Dark storm clouds with flat tops that resemble anvils.*

**3.** Cold air descends below the warm air and forces it upward.

**4.** Lead-colored cumulonimbus clouds cause heavy rains along the whole of the front.

**5.** The uppermost part of these clouds are often anvil-shaped.

# Thunder and Lightning

During a storm, powerful up-currents in the clouds cause water droplets and ice crystals to crash into each other. As a result, static electricity is produced inside the cloud. The upper parts of the cloud are positively charged, while the lower parts of the cloud are negatively charged. The base of the cloud is attracted to earth (normally positive), and the electricity in the cloud is discharged in the form of a bolt of lightning.

The energy contained in a lightning bolt heats the air surrounding it, causing it to expand quickly and to explode. This is the sound we know as thunder. Sound travels more slowly than light, so we see the lightning before we hear the thunder. You can easily calculate at what distance a lightning bolt has struck: Count the seconds between seeing the lightning and hearing the thunder and then multiply that by five. The answer will be the distance in miles from where you are to where the bolt struck. (If you wish to do this in meters, simply count the seconds, then multiply by 340.)

Lightning has so much energy that the air temperature around a lightning bolt can reach over 54,000°F (30,000°C).

1. Positive charges.
2. Negative charges.

3. The initial charge is like a spark for the lightning.
4. Negative charges from the cloud.

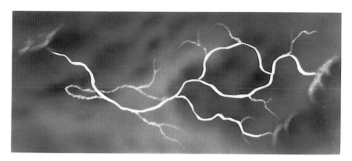

Lightning is formed when there is an electrical discharge between two clouds or different points of the same cloud.

Lightning always follows the shortest and easiest route from the cloud to the ground. So, if you get caught in a storm, make sure you avoid the highest places.

Lightning in a ball shape is a slow-moving sphere of electrical formation.

5. Positive charges from the ground to the cloud. It can generate up to 100 million volts of energy.

6. Shock waves that cause the thunder, which can be heard from long distances away.

# Clouds Climb Mountains

What happens if an air mass runs into a mountain range during its travels?

When air masses travel horizontally, they are likely to come across mountain ranges and be forced to rise. This ascent causes the air to cool and the water vapor in the cloud to condense. Clouds form on the side of the mountain that faces the wind. If the cloud has cooled sufficiently, rain will fall on this section of the mountain.

However, when the air mass reaches the other side of the mountain, it has usually lost all its water vapor and becomes more compact, warming up as it descends on the other side. The result is that in the lee of many great mountain ranges there is a "rain shadow" which can cause the formation of a desert. One example of this phenomenon is the great Patagonian desert, formed in the lee of the Andes Mountains.

Rain caused by clouds cooling as they are forced up the sides of a mountain range is called "orographic rainfall."

1. Warm, humid air.
2. The air rises and gradually cools down.

Deserts often form in the lee of large mountain ranges, as the mountains prevent water vapor from reaching the lee side.

The side of the mountain facing the wind (shown at the right) receives practically all of the rain.

During the night, the layer of air closest to the ground cools down to form dew.

**3.** Water vapor condenses as the air mass cools.

**4.** Heavy rain on the side of the mountain exposed to the wind.

# Snow on Mountaintops

As clouds rise up a mountainside, heavy snow falls on the mountaintops. Snow falls when the air is cold enough for snowflakes to reach the ground without melting. The heaviest snowfalls occur when the air temperature is around 32°F (0°C). This may seem strange, but if it is "too cold" (many degrees below the freezing temperature), it will not snow because colder air contains less humidity.

The snow that falls may form different shapes: stars, prisms, needles, sheets, etc.

Each form depends on the degree of humidity in the air.

Snow normally falls in flakes that are formed when ice crystals moisten, collide, and refreeze together in one larger flake. However, if the temperature is too low, the ice crystals will not join as they are too dry.

You will probably have noticed that precipitation begins as rain (when the temperature is around 37°F to 39°F) but as the temperature approaches 32°F, the rain gives way to sleet. Sometimes, falling snow melts just as it reaches ground level and turns to rain. What a shame!

The size and form of snow crystals depend on various factors: height, saturation levels in the cloud, and temperature. Crystals formed at low temperatures develop into prisms, while flakes form at higher temperatures. The ice crystals that form in clouds are relatively heavy. They grow in size as they fall.

## THE FORMATION OF AN AVALANCHE

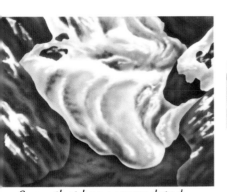

**1.** Various layers of snow accumulate.

**2.** The topmost layer fractures.

**3.** The entire mass moves down the mountainside.

*Snow that has accumulated on mountain summits may turn into ice and flow down into the valleys in the form of glaciers.*

*Lenticular clouds are lens-shaped and formed on the mountainsides facing the wind. Sometimes they have been mistaken for flying saucers!*

**1.** Snowflakes can take on an infinite combination of forms. However, they all have six sides and are formed by ice crystals.

**2.** Strong winds often blow on mountaintops. Even on sunny days, they make it feel colder than it really is.

# Bad Weather at Sea

What happens when a depression is located over the ocean?

A depression passing over the sea follows the sequence we have already described. In addition, however, the wind's force may create large waves, which may in turn endanger shipping and coastal zones.

The wind blows in the ships' sails, waves stand up as threatening walls of water, and heavy rain cuts visibility to almost zero. It has always been very important for sailors to know how to interpret the "signs" in the sky, allowing them to predict the likelihood of storms or favorable winds. In the past, ships were informed of the weather by means of a code of cylinders and cones placed on high points along the coastline. Today, they can listen to weather bulletins on the radio.

Ships are usually equipped with barometers and thermometers that provide information on atmospheric changes.

1

Bad weather at sea means rain and wind as well as heavy seas, which can cause great damage to the coast and ships at sea. The height of the waves depends on wind strength, its duration, and the distance of open sea that the wind has blown across.

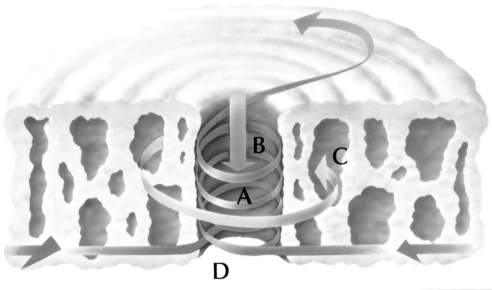

Hurricane winds can reach up to 149 miles per hour (240 km/hour).
**A.** Eye of the hurricane.
**B.** Falling air.
**C.** Winds spinning at great velocity.
**D.** Spiral bands of rain.

When a tornado forms over the sea, it becomes an enormous sea whirlwind.

**1.** You can easily see from a ship on the sea how a storm progresses.

**2.** When it rains heavily, the visibility is greatly reduced.

**3.** The wind can create waves several feet high.

# The Sky Clears

The weather improves quickly as a cold front moves away. If you look at the sky, you'll see that the clouds are clearing. After the cumulonimbus clouds have disappeared, altocumulus and then cumulus clouds appear, and then finally clearer patches begin to dominate the sky.

Once a cold front has passed over, the barometer will indicate that the atmospheric pressure is rising steadily, although the temperature will remain stable or tend to fall slightly (you'll notice that it's a bit colder).

The wind will drop but it will continue coming from the same direction, and the relative humidity will also decrease. The passing of a cold front is especially noticeable in cities because it "cleans the air" and leaves behind excellent visibility.

At sea, once the sky clears and the sun comes out, even though the wind has dropped, heavy waves still reach the shore. This swell is caused by large waves originating from storms far offshore. These waves may continue for some days after a fierce storm.

Even if there are still signs of bad weather, when the hand of the barometer gradually rises (as you can see on the left), it is an indication that good weather is coming.

## INLAND FOG

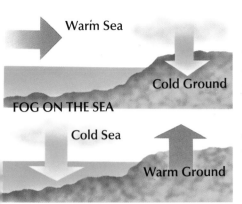

Warm Sea

Cold Ground

**FOG ON THE SEA**

Cold Sea

Warm Ground

*On the left, you can see how fog is formed when a humid air mass cools close to the ground or the sea's surface.*

*Small deposits of water droplets can sometimes be found at the base of some clouds after a storm. They are called mamatocumulus.*

3

A

B

C

C

**1.** The sky is clear.

**2.** There is a sea swell.

**3.** A rainbow is formed when the sun's rays cross through the water droplets. The droplets refract the rays and the white light splits into red, orange, yellow, green, blue, indigo, and purple. A. Sun's ray; B. Raindrop; C. Rainbow.

# Glossary

**Atmosphere:** The layer of gases surrounding the earth.

**Atmospheric pressure:** The pressure that the atmosphere's air has on the earth's surface.

**Coalescence:** The process in which little drops in the cloud start to fall and crash with each other to form bigger ones.

**Condensation:** The conversion of water from steam to liquid.

**Convection cells:** Circulation system of air in the atmosphere where the air of tropical regions is replaced with cold air from the polar regions.

**Coriolis force:** Due to the earth's rotation, it is when the wind's path or the path of a moving object changes from a straight line to a curve.

**Cubic meter:** The unit of volume equal to a cube whose side is one meter long. It is equivalent to 1000 liters.

**Dew point:** The maximum amount of water steam in the air at the lowest temperature possible where the water does not condense and turn into dew.

**Evaporation:** The transformation of a liquid into a gas, such as water into steam.

**Haze:** Another name for fog.

**Hemisphere:** Each half (northern or southern) of the earth.

**Lee:** In a mountain, it is the part that is protected from the wind.

**Millibar:** The unit of atmospheric pressure.

**Molecule:** A group of atoms that has all the properties of the substance it came from.

**Static electricity:** Due to the distribution of negative and positive charges, this is the electricity obtained when friction is applied to an object, or the electricity in a cloud before it is released as lightning.

**Water steam:** The name for water when it is gas.

# Index